written and illustrated by:

KATIE DAUGHERTY & LORA DIFRANCO

Free Period Press

www.freeperiodpress.com

HEY FRIEND, WELCOME!

WE ALL HAVE **A LOT** OF WORK TO DO TO CREATE A MORE *Loving* AND **JUST** WORLD, BUT YOU CAN'T TAKE CARE OF OTHERS UNLESS YOU'RE TAKING CARE OF YOURSELF. WE'VE COLLECTED SOME OF OUR **FAVORITE** THINGS THAT CHEER US UP WHEN WE'RE FEELING BLEH. IN THIS HANDY GUIDE WE'VE EVEN LEFT SOME SPACES TO ADD YOUR OWN FAVORITE THINGS THAT MAKE YOU UNIQUELY HAPPY.

Love,
KATIE & LORA

ADD
something
AWESOME
TO YOUR HOME

a

watch
Amélie

ask for
HELP

animal videos

FILL IN YOUR OWN FAVORITES HERE:

_____

_____

_____

CORGI BUTTS
CORGI BUTTS
CORGI BUTTS
CORGI BUTTS
CORGI BUTTS
CORGI BUTTS

BAKE *breathe deeply* **B**

GOOGLE "corgi butt"

have —a— BATH

BROWSE YOUR LOCAL BOOKSTORE

FILL IN YOUR OWN FAVORITES HERE:

_____

_____

_____

WATCH *the* CLOUDS

clean your room

CUDDLE with your PET or HUMAN companion

COLOR
SOMETHING FUN

WORK ON A CROSSWORD PUZZLE

MAKE **a cup of** COFFEE

C

light a candle

COLLAGE

compliment a stranger
(but not in like, a catcall way)

FILL IN YOUR OWN FAVORITES HERE:

_____

_____

_____

DOODLE
A LIL'
DOG HERE!

① ② ③ ④

Dance it Out

(may we suggest
"Water Fountain"
by tUnE-yArDs?)

DESSERT #2 anyone?

donate
to a cause
you care about

FILL IN YOUR OWN FAVORITES HERE:

_____

_____

_____

EXERCISE!

(or exercise your right not to...)

E

empty
your closet of everything you don't wear

enjoy
SILLY THINGS

FILL IN YOUR OWN FAVORITES HERE:

_____

_____

_____

acknowledge your *feelings*

BUILD a *fire*

SURROUND YOURSELF with FRIENDS & FAMILY

make a BLANKET FORT

FILL IN YOUR OWN FAVORITES HERE:

_____

_____

_____

I AM *grateful* FOR

GO TO -THE- gym

G

write down WHAT YOU'RE grateful FOR

garden

FILL IN YOUR OWN FAVORITES HERE:

_____

_____

_____

Local Parks to hike:

_____

_____

_____

_____

_____

_____

_____

_____

HELP
SOMEONE

host a
craft
night

GO FOR A
hike

FILL IN YOUR OWN FAVORITES HERE:

_____

_____

_____

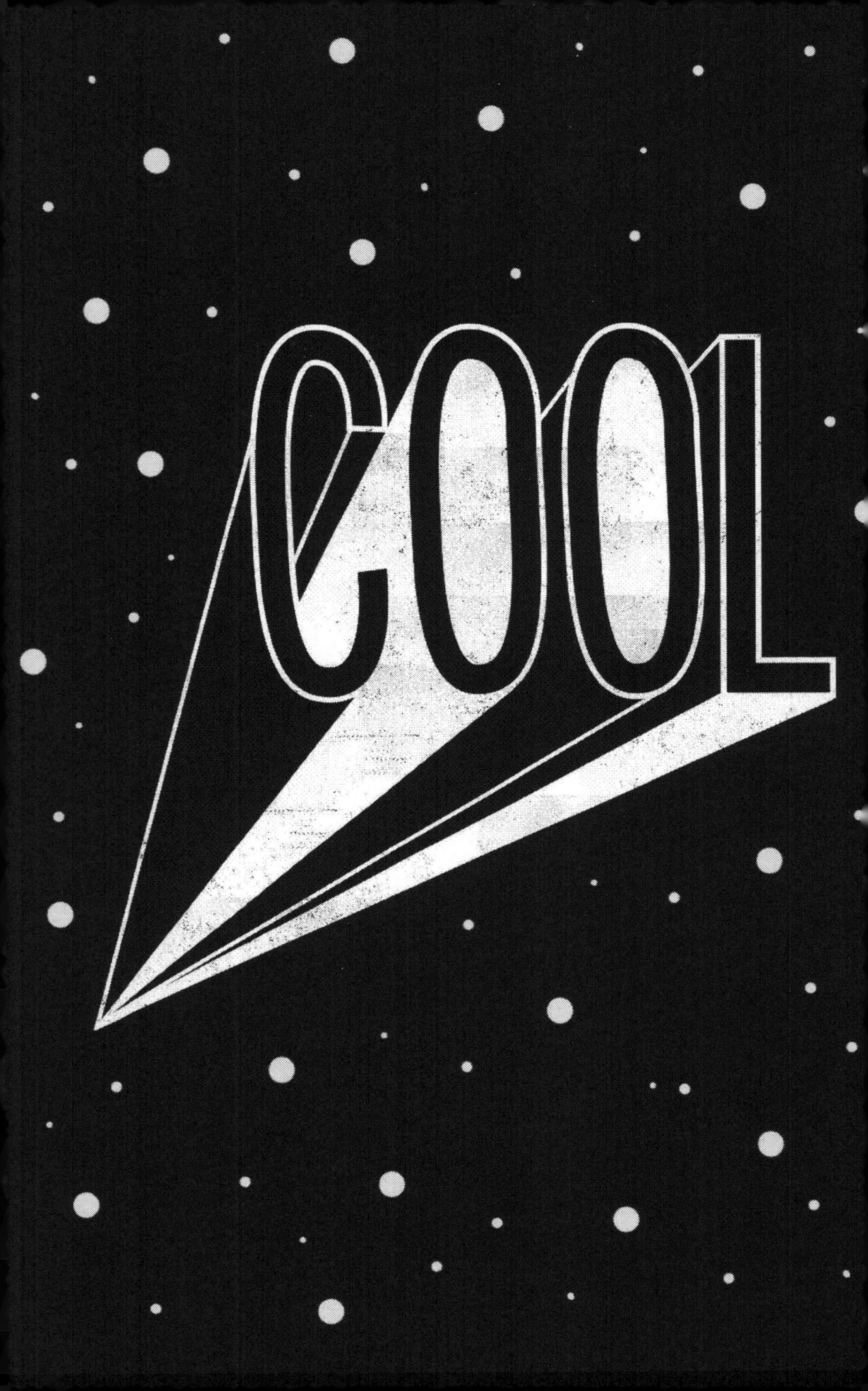
COOL

LISTEN TO AN INTERESTING INTERVIEW

text a friend AN INSIDE joke

ice cream sundaes

FILL IN YOUR OWN FAVORITES HERE:

_____

_____

_____

WHAT KINDS OF GROUPS WOULD YOU BE INTERESTED IN JOINING?

_____

_____

_____

_____

_____

_____

_____

IF YOU CAN'T FIND ONE TO JOIN, TRY STARTING YOUR OWN!

Journal J

JOIN
a FUN GROUP
(BOOKCLUB, SPORTS TEAM, KNITTING CIRCLE, ETC.)

JUMP
ON A
TRAMPOLINE

FILL IN YOUR OWN FAVORITES HERE:

_____

_____

_____

knit a **FUZZY** Scarf

KISS SOMEONE/ SOMETHING **YOU LOVE**

VIDEOS

FILL IN YOUR OWN FAVORITES HERE:

_____

_____

_____

LIST OF TOPICS YOU'RE INTERESTED IN AND WOULD LIKE TO LEARN MORE ABOUT:

_____

_____

_____

_____

_____

_____

_____

_____

OUR LIST INCLUDES MOROCCAN TILES, RURAL ECONOMICS, AND LANDSCAPE ARCHITECTURE.

visit your LOCAL LIBRARY

L

send A LETTER

learn SOMETHING new

Listen TO A NEW BAND

FILL IN YOUR OWN FAVORITES HERE:

_____

_____

_____

MEDITATE

Call your ♥ mom

BUY & READ A NEW
Magazine
THAT CATCHES YOUR EYE

visit a
MUSEUM

GET A
massage

watch
Your
favorite
MOVIE

MOISTURIZE!

FILL IN YOUR OWN FAVORITES HERE:

_____

_____

_____

REST

take a DANG nap

PAINT YOUR NAILS

TRY new FOOD!

FILL IN YOUR OWN FAVORITES HERE:

_____

_____

_____

GET
COZY

talk to an
octogenarian

ORDER
yummy
TAKEOUT

ORGANIZE
your
DESK

FILL IN YOUR OWN FAVORITES HERE:

_____

_____

_____

host
— a —
POTLUCK

Paint

P

PRAY

GO ON A
PhOToGRaPhy
WALK

LOOK at

FAMILY
PHOTO
ALBUMS

Listen TO A
PODCAST

FILL IN YOUR OWN FAVORITES HERE:

_____

_____

_____

QUOTE a FUNNY MOVIE

Q

QUIT worrying for 5 minutes

FILL IN YOUR OWN FAVORITES HERE:

_____

_____

_____

RELAX
FOR A
DANG
MINUTE

READ

relax

PUT on a RECORD

GO FOR A Run

FILL IN YOUR OWN FAVORITES HERE:

_____

_____

_____

wear your
comfiest
sweater

Listen
TO YOUR
FAVORITE
song

PUT ON YOUR
**BRIGHEST
SPANDEX**
& EMBRACE YOUR INNER
MODERN DANCER

stret

ATTEND a
SPORTING
EVENT
(FACEPAINT OPTIONAL)

SLEEP FOR 8 HOUURS

watch your favorite stand-up comedian

Watch the sunrise —or— sunset

hhhhhhhhhh

FILL IN YOUR OWN FAVORITES HERE:

_____

_____

_____

HAVE A SPOT 🍵 OF

TEA

tidy UP

write a thank you note

TRAVEL

FILL IN YOUR OWN FAVORITES HERE:

_____

_____

_____

unplug.

for **1** hour.

right now.

FILL IN YOUR OWN FAVORITES HERE:

_____

_____

_____

CIRCLE THE CAUSES YOU WANT TO VOLUNTEER FOR:

SPEND 15 MINUTES SEARCHING FOR LOCAL
ORGANIZATIONS THAT DEAL WITH THESE ISSUES.

DRUG ABUSE

COMMUNITY DEVELOPMENT

VETERANS

HEALTH

ARTS

ANIMALS

EDUCATION

IMMIGRATION

PRISON REFORM

YOUTH

LGBTQ

OLDER ADULTS

DISABILITIES

_____

_____

VISIT an **OLD FRIEND**

VOLUNTEER

PLAY YOUR FAVORITE **VIDEO GAME**

FILL IN YOUR OWN FAVORITES HERE:

_____

_____

_____

WRITE A STORY ABOUT A GIRL WEARING A GREEN HAT:

READ THE WORD of the DAY

SIT NEXT TO A BODY OF WATER & Listen

WALK & walk & walk & walk

HAVE A BIG OL' GLASS OF WATER
(WITH LEMON IF YOU'RE FEELING FANCY)

write STORY

FILL IN YOUR OWN FAVORITES HERE:

_____

_____

_____

DO SOME
YOGA
XY
&z

zone
out
for FOR A BIT

find your
zen

FILL IN YOUR OWN FAVORITES HERE:

_____

_____

_____

HERE'S MORE SPACE
FOR YOUR FAVORITES!

_____

_____

_____

_____

_____

_____

_____